Leif The Lion Education

4th Grade Math

A Christian Homeschool Guide

By Matthew E. Webb

Leif The Lion Education

4th Grade Math Christian Homeschool Guide

Dear Parents and Students,

Welcome to the 4th Grade Christian Homeschool Guide. This curriculum is designed to introduce or supplement essential math concepts from a Christian perspective.

Each lesson contains biblical truth, clear objectives, and manageable practice questions designed for independent learners. We believe that mathematics reveals God's order and faithfulness, and this guide encourages students to see God's hand in logic and learning.

This guide is designed to have minimal parent involvement within a simple structure that drives a reflection-based approach. This curriculum fosters both spiritual and academic growth. May God bless your learning journey!

In Christ,
Matthew E. Webb

Each lesson includes a biblical focus, math questions, and a reflection prompt.

The answers are included after each Unit.

Table of Contents

Unit 1: Place Value and Number Sense

- Understanding Place Value up to Millions
- Reading and Writing Large Numbers
- Comparing and Ordering Whole Numbers
- Rounding Numbers to the Nearest Ten, Hundred, and Thousand
- Exploring Patterns in Number Sequences

Unit 2: Addition and Subtraction

- Adding Large Numbers with Regrouping
- Subtracting Large Numbers with Regrouping
- Solving Multi-Step Word Problems
- Estimating Sums and Differences
- Checking for Reasonableness

Unit 3: Multiplication

- Multiplying by 1-Digit Numbers
- Multiplying by 2-Digit Numbers
- Properties of Multiplication
- Multiplication Word Problems
- Estimating Products

Unit 4: Division

- Understanding Division as Repeated Subtraction
- Division Facts and Strategies
- Dividing by 1-Digit Numbers
- Estimating Quotients

Leif The Lion Education

- Division Word Problems

Unit 5: Fractions

- Understanding Fractions as Part of a Whole
- Equivalent Fractions
- Comparing and Ordering Fractions
- Adding and Subtracting Like Fractions
- Understanding Mixed Numbers and Improper Fractions

Unit 6: Decimals

- Understanding Tenths and Hundredths
- Reading and Writing Decimals
- Comparing and Ordering Decimals
- Rounding Decimals
- Adding and Subtracting Decimals

Unit 7: Measurement

- Measuring Length (U.S. Customary and Metric)
- Measuring Weight and Mass
- Measuring Capacity
- Solving Measurement Word Problems
- Converting Units of Measurement

Leif The Lion Education

Unit 8: Geometry

- Identifying Points, Lines, and Angles
- Classifying Triangles and Quadrilaterals
- Lines of Symmetry
- Measuring Angles with a Protractor
- Perimeter and Area

Unit 9: Data and Graphing

- Reading Pictographs and Bar Graphs
- Creating Line Plots and Frequency Tables
- Interpreting Line Graphs
- Organizing Data
- Mean, Median, Mode, and Range

Unit 10: Patterns and Algebraic Thinking

- Identifying Patterns and Sequences
- Solving for Unknowns in Equations
- Writing and Evaluating Expressions
- Using Input-Output Tables
- Problem Solving with Patterns

Unit 1
PLACE VALUE AND NUMBER SENSE

 Understanding Place Value up to Millions

- Reading and Writing Large Numbers

- Comparing and Ordering Whole Numbers

- Rounding Numbers to the Nearest Ten, Hundred, and Thousand

- Exploring Patterns in Number Sequences

Leif The Lion Education

Lesson 1: Understanding Place Value up to Millions

Biblical Focus:

"Let all things be done decently and in order." – 1 Corinthians 14:40 God values order in all aspects of creation. Just as numbers must be placed correctly to have value, our lives have purpose when we are aligned with God's order.

Lesson Objective:

Students will learn to identify the value of each digit in a number up to the millions place and understand how the position of a digit affects its value.

Example:

Look at the number **4,382,615**.

- The digit **4** is in the millions place. It represents **4,000,000**.

- The digit **3** is in the hundred-thousandth place. It represents **300,000**.

- The digit **8** is in the ten-thousandth place. It represents **80,000**.

- The digit **2** is in the thousands place. It represents **2,000**.

- The digit **6** is in the hundreds place. It represents **600**.

- The digit **1** is in the tens place. It represents **10**.

- The digit **5** is in the ones place. It represents **5**.

Each digit's value depends on its place. Without the correct place value, the number would be confusing or meaningless.

Leif The Lion Education

Practice Problems:

1. Write the value of the underlined digit: **7**,539,821

2. What is the value of the digit **6** in the number 2,**6**85,934?

3. Which digit is in the ten-thousandths place in the number 983,241?

4. Write this number in expanded form: 4,102,307

5. Identify the place value of the digit **9** in the number 5,794,112

Reflection:

Take a moment to review the Biblical focus for this section. What does that Bible verse mean to you, and how can you live it or relate to the math concepts learned in this lesson?

_____

_____

_____

_____

_____

Lesson 2: Reading and Writing Large Numbers

Biblical Focus:

"Write the vision, and make it plain upon tables, that he may run that readeth it." – Habakkuk 2:2

God encourages clarity and understanding. Just as we must write and read His Word clearly, we must also learn to read and write numbers correctly for them to be understood.

Lesson Objective:

Students will learn to read and write numbers in standard form, word form, and expanded form up to millions.

Example:

Number: **3,407,025**

- **Standard Form**: 3,407,025

- **Word Form**: Three million, four hundred seven thousand, twenty-five

- **Expanded Form**: 3,000,000 + 400,000 + 7,000 + 20 + 5

Each form shows the same value differently. Understanding all three helps build a stronger number sense.

Practice Problems:

1. Write 6,812,094 in word form.

2. Write the number **five million, thirty thousand, two hundred four** in standard form.

Leif The Lion Education

3. Write 2,104,300 in expanded form.

4. Write the number **seven million, five hundred thousand, nine** in standard form.

5. Convert this expanded form to standard form: 5,000,000 + 600,000 + 20,000 + 100 + 2

Reflection:

Take a moment to review the Biblical focus for this section. What does that Bible verse mean to you, and how can you live it or relate to the math concepts learned in this lesson?

_____

_____

_____

_____

_____

Lesson 3: Comparing and Ordering Whole Numbers

Biblical Focus:

"Better is a little with righteousness than great revenues without right." – Proverbs 16:8
This verse teaches us that value is not always about size, but about meaning and righteousness. In math, comparing numbers is about understanding value, not just seeing which is bigger.

Lesson Objective:

Students will learn how to compare and order whole numbers up to the millions using place value, greater than (>), less than (<), and equal to (=) symbols.

Example:

Compare 5,234,810 and 5,243,110

- Start by comparing digits from left to right:

  - Millions: 5 vs 5 → same

  - Hundred Thousands: 2 vs 2 → same

  - Ten Thousands: 3 vs 4 → 3 < 4
    So, **5,234,810 < 5,243,110**

Ordering Example:

Put in order from least to greatest:
4,100,050 – 3,999,999 – 4,100,005
Answer: 3,999,999 < 4,100,005 < 4,100,050

Leif The Lion Education

Practice Problems:

1. Compare: 6,120,400 ___ 6,102,300

2. Use >, <, or =: 9,876,321 ___ 9,876,231

3. Order from least to greatest: 7,450,000 – 7,405,000 – 7,540,000

4. Order from greatest to least: 1,234,567 – 1,234,765 – 1,234,675

5. Compare: 8,000,000 ___ 7,999,999

Reflection:

Take a moment to review the Biblical focus for this section. What does that Bible verse mean to you, and how can you live it or relate to the math concepts learned in this lesson?

_____

_____

_____

Lesson 4: Rounding Numbers to the Nearest Ten, Hundred, and Thousand

Biblical Focus:

"Teach us to number our days, that we may gain a heart of wisdom." – Psalm 90:12

Just like rounding helps us simplify and plan more easily in math, this verse reminds us that we must be wise with the time and numbers in our lives, making each one count.

Lesson Objective:

Students will learn how to round numbers to the nearest ten, hundred, and thousand using place value.

Example:

To round **4,372** to the nearest hundred:

- Look at the tens digit (7). Since it is 5 or more, round the hundreds digit up.

- 4,372 rounded to the nearest hundred is **4,400**

To round **4,372** to the nearest thousand:

- Look at the hundreds digit (3). Since it is less than 5, round down.

- 4,372 rounded to the nearest thousand is **4,000**

Leif The Lion Education

Practice Problems:

1. Round 6,849 to the nearest ten.

2. Round 9,231 to the nearest hundred.

3. Round 5,672 to the nearest thousand.

4. Round 3,965 to the nearest hundred.

5. Round 8,205 to the nearest thousand.

Reflection:

Take a moment to review the Biblical focus for this section. What does that Bible verse mean to you, and how can you live it or relate to the math concepts learned in this lesson?

_____

_____

_____

Lesson 5: Exploring Patterns in Number Sequences

Biblical Focus:

"For everything there is a season, and a time for every matter under heaven." –
Ecclesiastes 3:1

God created the world with order and rhythm. Patterns in math reflect the patterns we see in nature and in God's timing—predictable, purposeful, and meaningful.

Lesson Objective:

Students will learn to identify, continue, and create number patterns using addition, subtraction, multiplication, and division.

Example:

Pattern: 3, 6, 12, 24, 48,?

- Each number is multiplied by 2

- The next number is **96**

Another Pattern: 100, 90, 80, 70,?

- Each number decreases by 10

- The next number is **60**

Practice Problems:

1. What are the next two numbers? 5, 10, 15, 20, ____, ____

2. Fill in the missing number: 2, 4, ____, 16, 32

3. Describe the pattern: 81, 72, 63, 54

4. Create your pattern that increases by 3. Write the first 5 numbers.

5. What is the rule for this pattern: 100, 50, 25, 12.5?

Reflection:

Take a moment to review the Biblical focus for this section. What does that Bible verse mean to you, and how can you live it or relate to the math concepts learned in this lesson?

_____

_____

_____

Leif The Lion Education

Answer Key for Unit 1: Place Value and Number Sense

Lesson 1: Understanding Place Value up to Millions

1. **7,000,000** – The digit 7 is in the millions place.

2. **600,000** – The digit 6 is in the hundred-thousandth place.

3. **8** – The digit 8 is in the ten thousands place.

4. **4,000,000 + 100,000 + 2,000 + 300 + 0 + 0 + 7** – Expanded form.

5. **Hundred thousands place** – The digit 9 is in that place and has a value of **900,000**.

Lesson 2: Reading and Writing Large Numbers

1. **Six million, eight hundred twelve thousand, ninety-four** – This is the word form of 6,812,094.

2. **5,030,204** – This is the standard form of the number written in words.

3. **2,000,000 + 100,000 + 4,000 + 300** – Expanded form of 2,104,300.

Leif The Lion Education

4. **7,500,009** – This is the standard form of "Seven million, five hundred thousand, nine."

5. **5,620,102** – Combine the values from the expanded form: 5,000,000 + 600,000 + 20,000 + 100 + 2.

Lesson 3: Comparing and Ordering Whole Numbers

1. **<** – 6,120,400 is less than 6,102,300.

2. **>** – 9,876,321 is greater than 9,876,231.

3. **7,405,000 < 7,450,000 < 7,540,000** – Order from least to greatest.

4. **1,234,765 > 1,234,675 > 1,234,567** – Order from greatest to least.

5. **>** – 8,000,000 is greater than 7,999,999.

Lesson 4: Rounding Numbers to the Nearest Ten, Hundred, and Thousand

1. **6,850** – Round 6,849 to the nearest ten (the ones digit is 9, so round up).

2. **9,200** – Round 9,231 to the nearest hundred (tens digit is 3, round down).

3. **6,000** – Round 5,672 to the nearest thousand (hundred's digit is 6, round up).

4. **4,000** – Round 3,965 to the nearest hundred, then to the nearest thousand.

5. **8,000** – Round 8,205 to the nearest thousand (hundred's digit is 2, round down).

Lesson 5: Exploring Patterns in Number Sequences

1. **25, 30** – Add 5 each time.

2. **8** – The missing number is 8 in the pattern: 2, 4, 8, 16, 32 (multiply by 2).

3. **Subtract 9** – Pattern: 81, 72, 63, 54 (decreasing by 9).

4. **3, 6, 9, 12, 15** – Create a pattern by adding 3.

5. **Divide by 2** – Pattern rule: 100, 50, 25, 12.5 (dividing by 2 each time).

Leif The Lion Education

UNIT 2:
ADDITION AND SUBTRACTION

	HUNDREDS	TENS	ONES
+	4	5	8

 Adding Large Numbers with Regrouping

 Subtracting Large Numbers with Regrouping

 Solving Multi-Step Word Problems

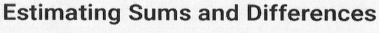 Estimating Sums and Differences

 Checking for Reasonableness

WISDOM BEGINS WITH GOD

Leif The Lion Education

Lesson 1: Adding Large Numbers with Regrouping

Biblical Focus:

"Every good and perfect gift is from above, coming down from the Father of the heavenly lights." – James 1:17

Just as each digit in addition builds upon the next, every blessing in our life builds upon the grace of God. Adding with care reminds us of the careful attention God gives to us.

Lesson Objective:

Students will learn how to add large whole numbers using place value strategies and regrouping when sums exceed 9 in a given column.

Example:

Add 24,358 + 19,876

1. Start from the right (ones place): 8 + 6 = 14 → write 4, carry 1

2. Tens: 5 + 7 = 12, plus 1 = 13 → write 3, carry 1

3. Hundreds: 3 + 8 = 11, plus 1 = 12 → write 2, carry 1

4. Thousands: 4 + 9 = 13, plus 1 = 14 → write 4, carry 1

5. Ten-thousands: 2 + 1 = 3, plus 1 = 4
   Answer: 44,234

Practice Problems:

1. Add: 24,138 + 29,338

2. Add: 53,872 + 46,249

3. Add: 71,901 + 57,103

4. Add: 35,402 + 41,430

5. Add: 478,329 + 412,371

Reflection:

Take a moment to review the Biblical focus for this section. What does that Bible verse mean to you, and how can you live it or relate to the math concepts learned in this lesson?

_____

_____

_____

Leif The Lion Education

Lesson 2: Subtracting Large Numbers with Regrouping

Biblical Focus:

"The Lord is not slow in keeping his promise, as some understand slowness. Instead, he is patient with you." – 2 Peter 3:9

Subtraction takes patience and care, especially when regrouping. Just like God is patient with us, we must be patient with each step in solving problems.

Lesson Objective:

Students will learn to subtract large numbers with regrouping across multiple place values.

Example:

Subtract: 62,305 − 27,489

1. Start at the ones place: 5 − 9 → regroup

2. Continue regrouping as needed through tens, hundreds, etc.
   Answer: 34,816

Practice Problems:

1. Subtract: 85,901 − 43,223

2. Subtract: 97,632 − 46,423

Leif The Lion Education

3. Subtract: 74,509 − 6,488

4. Subtract: 198,750 − 75,350

5. Subtract: 123,600 − 44,700

Reflection:

Take a moment to review the Biblical focus for this section. What does that Bible verse mean to you, and how can you live it or relate to the math concepts learned in this lesson?

_____

_____

_____

_____

_____

Lesson 3: Solving Multi-Step Word Problems

Biblical Focus:

"Commit to the Lord whatever you do, and he will establish your plans." – Proverbs 16:3
Solving multi-step problems teaches planning and trust in the process. When we commit to doing each part carefully, we reflect the order and purpose that God brings to our lives.

Lesson Objective:

Students will solve word problems requiring two or more steps using addition and subtraction.

Example:

Sophia has 125 marbles. She gives 38 to her brother and buys 64 more. How many marbles does she have now?

Step 1: 125 − 38 = 87
Step 2: 87 + 64 = **151 marbles**

Practice Problems:

1. David has 230 stickers. He gives away 75, then buys 40 more. How many does he have now?

2. A library has 6,200 books. 1,345 are borrowed. Then, 250 new books are added. How many are now in the library?

3. You walk 1,250 steps before lunch and 1,475 after. Then you rest and walk 600 more. What's your total?

4. A store sold 900 items in June and 1,050 in July. If 600 were returned, how many stayed sold?

5. A family drives 325 miles to a vacation, then drives 130 miles to another site, then back 455 miles home. What is the total distance?

Reflection:

Take a moment to review the Biblical focus for this section. What does that Bible verse mean to you, and how can you live it or relate to the math concepts learned in this lesson?

_____

_____

_____

_____

_____

Lesson 4: Estimating Sums and Differences

Biblical Focus:

"Plans fail for lack of counsel, but with many advisers they succeed." – Proverbs 15:22

Estimation is a wise strategy, like advice before acting. It helps us stay on track and avoid mistakes. It teaches us to think carefully before jumping to conclusions.

Lesson Objective:

Students will estimate sums and differences by rounding to the nearest ten, hundred, or thousand.

Example:

Estimate 4,283 + 2,715

Round: 4,283 → 4,000 and 2,715 → 3,000

Estimate: **7,000**

Practice Problems:

1. Estimate: 25,678 + 34,591

2. Estimate: 78,921 − 45,204

3. Estimate: 16,295 + 42,607

4. Estimate: 93,745 − 38,301

Leif The Lion Education

5. Estimate: 6,049 + 3,980

Reflection:

Take a moment to review the Biblical focus for this section. What does that Bible verse mean to you, and how can you live it or relate to the math concepts learned in this lesson?

_____

_____

_____

_____

_____

Lesson 5: Checking for Reasonableness

Biblical Focus:

"Do not merely listen to the word, and so deceive yourselves. Do what it says." – James 1:22

Just as we must live according to God's Word, we must also check that our actions—and our math—are correct. Reasonableness helps us stay honest and accurate.

Lesson Objective:

Students will learn to check their answers using estimation, inverse operations, and logic to decide if an answer is reasonable.

Example:

Problem: 34,190 + 28,407 = 62,597

Estimate: 34,000 + 28,000 = 62,000 → The answer is reasonable.

Check with subtraction: 62,597 − 28,407 = 34,190 → Confirmed.

Practice Problems:

1. Estimate and check: 45,728 + 12,104 = 57,832

2. Estimate and check: 99,605 − 47,288 = 52,317

3. Check if this is reasonable: 18,200 + 5,639 = 12,561

4. Use subtraction to check: 64,700 + 9,125 = 73,825

5. Round and verify: 7,346 + 2,208 = 9,554

Reflection:

Take a moment to review the Biblical focus for this section. What does that Bible verse mean to you, and how can you live it or relate to the math concepts learned in this lesson?

_____

_____

_____

_____

_____

Answer Key for Unit 2: Addition and Subtraction

Lesson 1: Adding Large Numbers with Regrouping

1. **24,138 + 29,338 = 53,476**

   Add each column right to left, regroup where sums exceed 9.

2. **53,872 + 46,249 = 100,121**

   Carry over from the thousands and tens columns while adding place by place.

3. **71,901 + 57,103 = 129,004**

   Align digits and add; regroup across hundreds and thousands.

4. **35,402 + 41,430 = 76,832**

   Add each digit column, regrouping in tens and hundreds.

5. **478,329 + 412,371 = 890,700**

   Add each place value, regrouping hundreds and thousands to get the correct sum.

Lesson 2: Subtracting Large Numbers with Regrouping

1. **85,901 − 43,223 = 42,678**

   Regroup starting at the ones column; subtract each digit.

2. **97,632 − 46,423 = 51,209**

   Subtract digit by digit, borrowing from the next left column when needed.

Leif The Lion Education

3. **74,509 − 6,488 = 68,021**

   Regroup across tens, hundreds, and thousands to complete subtraction.

4. **198,750 − 75,350 = 123,400**

   Subtract digits from right to left with regrouping across place values.

5. **123,600 − 44,700 = 78,900**

   Straightforward subtraction with some regrouping in hundreds and thousands.

Lesson 3: Solving Multi-Step Word Problems

1. **230 − 75 + 40 = 195 stickers**

   First, subtract 75, then add 40 to find the total.

2. **6,200 − 1,345 + 250 = 5,105 books**

   Subtract borrowed books, then add the new ones.

3. **1,250 + 1,475 + 600 = 3,325 steps**

   Add all steps taken during different parts of the day.

4. **900 + 1,050 − 600 = 1,350 items**

   Add both months' sales, then subtract returns.

5. **325 + 130 + 455 = 910 miles**

   Add up each leg of the trip to get the total distance traveled.

Leif The Lion Education

Lesson 4: Estimating Sums and Differences

1. **25,678 → 26,000; 34,591 → 35,000 → 26,000 + 35,000 = 61,000 (estimated sum)**

2. **78,921 → 79,000; 45,204 → 45,000 → 79,000 − 45,000 = 34,000 (estimated difference)**

3. **16,295 → 16,000; 42,607 → 43,000 → 16,000 + 43,000 = 59,000**

4. **93,745 → 94,000; 38,301 → 38,000 → 94,000 − 38,000 = 56,000**

5. **6,049 → 6,000; 3,980 → 4,000 → 6,000 + 4,000 = 10,000**

Lesson 5: Checking for Reasonableness

1. **45,728 + 12,104 = 57,832**
   Estimate: 46,000 + 12,000 = 58,000 → Close, so reasonable.

2. **99,605 − 47,288 = 52,317**
   Estimate: 100,000 − 47,000 = 53,000 → Close match, reasonable.

3. **18,200 + 5,639 = 23,839**
   Estimate: 18,000 + 6,000 = 24,000 → Actual is close, so reasonable.

4. **64,700 + 9,125 = 73,825 → Check: 73,825 − 9,125 = 64,700 → Confirmed**

5. **7,346 + 2,208 = 9,554 → Estimate: 7,000 + 2,000 = 9,000 → Close match**

UNIT 3: MULTIPLICATION

- Multiplying by 1-Digit Numbers
- Multiplying by 2-Digit Numbers
- Properties of Multiplication
- Properties of Muplication
- Multiplication Word Problems

$$\begin{array}{r} 27 \\ \times\ 6 \\ \hline 162 \end{array}$$

WORKSHEET

Leif The Lion Education

Lesson 1: Multiplying by 1-Digit Numbers

Biblical Focus:

"Whatever you do, work at it with all your heart, as working for the Lord, not for human masters." – Colossians 3:23

Even in basic work like multiplication, we honor God when we give our best. Effort in learning is part of worship.

Lesson Objective:

Students will multiply 1-digit numbers with fluency and accuracy using foundational multiplication facts.

Example:

Multiply: 7×6

Answer: 42

Explanation: Multiply 7 by 6 using memorized facts or repeated addition ($7 + 7 + 7 + 7 + 7 + 7 = 42$).

Practice Problems:

1. $6 \times 4 =$

2. $7 \times 8 =$

3. $9 \times 3 =$

4. 5 × 12 =

5. 8 × 7 =

Reflection:

Take a moment to review the Biblical focus for this section. What does that Bible verse mean to you, and how can you live it or relate to the math concepts learned in this lesson?

_____

_____

_____

_____

_____

Lesson 2: Multiplying by 2-Digit Numbers

Biblical Focus:

"Do you see a man skillful in his work? He will stand before kings." – Proverbs 22:29

Gaining skill, even in multiplication, is a form of discipline that leads to great opportunity. God blesses hard work.

Lesson Objective:

Students will learn to multiply 2-digit numbers by 1-digit numbers using place value strategies and partial products.

Example:

Multiply: 23×4

Step 1: $3 \times 4 = 12$

Step 2: $20 \times 4 = 80$

Final Answer: $12 + 80 = \mathbf{92}$

Practice Problems:

1. $23 \times 4 =$

2. $45 \times 6 =$

3. $12 \times 12 =$

4. 31 × 3 =

5. 18 × 5 =

Reflection:

Take a moment to review the Biblical focus for this section. What does that Bible verse mean to you, and how can you live it or relate to the math concepts learned in this lesson?

_____

_____

_____

_____

_____

Lesson 3: Properties of Multiplication

Leif The Lion Education

Biblical Focus:

"Jesus Christ is the same yesterday and today and forever." – Hebrews 13:8

Just as God is consistent and unchanging, the properties of multiplication are reliable and true in every situation.

Lesson Objective:

Students will identify and apply multiplication properties: Identity, Commutative, Associative, Zero, and Distributive.

Example:

Distributive Property:

$5 \times (6 + 2) = (5 \times 6) + (5 \times 2) = 30 + 10 = \mathbf{40}$

Practice Problems:

1. $6 \times 1 =$ (Which property?)

2. $3 \times 4 = 4 \times 3$ (Which property?)

3. $2 \times (3 \times 4) = (2 \times 3) \times 4$ (Which property?)

4. $7 \times 0 =$ (Which property?)

5. $5 \times (6 + 2) = (5 \times 6) + (5 \times 2)$ (Which property?)

Leif The Lion Education

Reflection:

Take a moment to review the Biblical focus for this section. What does that Bible verse mean to you, and how can you live it or relate to the math concepts learned in this lesson?

_____

_____

_____

_____

_____

Lesson 4: Multiplication Word Problems

Leif The Lion Education

Biblical Focus:

"Let all that you do be done in love." – 1 Corinthians 16:14

Math word problems can teach us to think critically and solve with care. When done with patience and love, even simple problems reflect God's way.

Lesson Objective:

Students will use multiplication to solve real-world word problems involving repeated groups and arrays.

Example:

There are 4 bags with 6 apples each.

Multiply: 4 × 6 = **24 apples**

Practice Problems:

1. A box holds 6 apples. How many apples are in 4 boxes?

2. There are 7 rows of 5 chairs. How many chairs?

3. A store sells 12 packs of pencils with 10 pencils each. How many total pencils?

4. If 3 people each read 8 pages, how many pages in total?

5. There are 9 baskets with 4 eggs in each. How many eggs?

Reflection:

Take a moment to review the Biblical focus for this section. What does that Bible verse mean to you, and how can you live it or relate to the math concepts learned in this lesson?

_____

_____

_____

_____

_____

Lesson 5: Estimating Products

Leif The Lion Education

Biblical Focus:

"The plans of the diligent lead surely to abundance, but everyone who is hasty comes only to poverty." – Proverbs 21:5

Estimation teaches us to plan with wisdom before solving. God values thoughtful, patient action.

Lesson Objective:

Students will estimate products by rounding factors to the nearest ten before multiplying.

Example:

Estimate 47 × 6

Round 47 to 50

50 × 6 = **300**

Practice Problems:

1. Estimate: 42 × 7

2. Estimate: 18 × 5

3. Estimate: 63 × 6

4. Estimate: 27 × 4

5. Estimate: 91 × 3

Reflection:

Take a moment to review the Biblical focus for this section. What does that Bible verse mean to you, and how can you live it or relate to the math concepts learned in this lesson?

_____

_____

_____

_____

_____

Lesson 1: Multiplying by 1-Digit Numbers

1. **6 × 4 = 24**

   Multiply 6 by 4 directly using multiplication facts.

2. **7 × 8 = 56**

   This is a basic times table fact: seven groups of eight equal 56.

3. **9 × 3 = 27**

   Multiply 9 by 3 using memorized facts or repeated addition.

4. **5 × 12 = 60**

   Multiply 5 by 12, or use 5 × 10 = 50 and 5 × 2 = 10, then add: 50 + 10 = 60.

5. **8 × 7 = 56**

   Multiply 8 by 7 directly from multiplication tables.

Lesson 2: Multiplying by 2-Digit Numbers

1. **23 × 4 = 92**

   Break apart 23 as 20 + 3. Multiply: 20 × 4 = 80, 3 × 4 = 12 → 80 + 12 = 92.

2. **45 × 6 = 270**

   Break into 40 × 6 = 240 and 5 × 6 = 30 → 240 + 30 = 270.

3. **12 × 12 = 144**

   This is a memorized square fact.

Leif The Lion Education

4. **31 × 3 = 93**

   Break into 30 × 3 = 90 and 1 × 3 = 3 → 90 + 3 = 93.

5. **18 × 5 = 90**

   Break into 10 × 5 = 50 and 8 × 5 = 40 → 50 + 40 = 90.

Lesson 3: Properties of Multiplication

1. **6 × 1 = 6**

   Identity Property: Any number times 1 equals itself.

2. **3 × 4 = 4 × 3**

   Commutative Property: Order does not affect the result.

3. **2 × (3 × 4) = (2 × 3) × 4 = 24**

   Associative Property: Grouping does not affect the result.

4. **7 × 0 = 0**

   Zero Property: Any number times zero equals zero.

5. **5 × (6 + 2) = (5 × 6) + (5 × 2) = 30 + 10 = 40**

   Distributive Property: Multiply across the sum in parentheses.

Lesson 4: Multiplication Word Problems

Leif The Lion Education

1. **4 × 6 = 24 apples**

   Four boxes with six apples each equals 24 total apples.

2. **7 × 5 = 35 chairs**

   Seven rows of five chairs equals 35 chairs.

3. **12 × 10 = 120 pencils**

   Twelve packs of 10 pencils equals 120 pencils.

4. **3 × 8 = 24 pages**

   Three people reading 8 pages each equals 24 pages total.

5. **9 × 4 = 36 eggs**

   Nine baskets, each holding four eggs, equals 36 eggs.

Lesson 5: Estimating Products

1. **42 × 7 ≈ 40 × 7 = 280**

   Round 42 to 40 for easier multiplication.

2. **18 × 5 ≈ 20 × 5 = 100**

   Round 18 to 20 to estimate quickly.

3. **63 × 6 ≈ 60 × 6 = 360**

   Round 63 to 60, then multiply.

4. **27 × 4 ≈ 30 × 4 = 120**

   Round 27 to 30 to estimate.

5. **91 × 3 ≈ 90 × 3 = 270**

    Round 91 to 90, then multiply.

UNIT 4
DIVISION

- **Understanding Division as Repeated Subtraction**
- **Division Facts and Strategies**
- **Dividing by 1-Digit Numbers**
- **Estimating Quotients**
- **Division Word Problems**

Lesson 1: Understanding Division as Repeated Subtraction

Biblical Focus:

"Let us not become weary in doing good, for at the proper time we will reap a harvest if we do not give up." – Galatians 6:9

Just like division through repeated subtraction takes patience, so does doing what is right. Keep going even when it takes effort.

Lesson Objective:

Students will understand division as repeated subtraction and connect it to real-world groupings.

Example:

Divide $12 \div 3$

Subtract 3 repeatedly: $12 - 3 = 9, 9 - 3 = 6, 6 - 3 = 3, 3 - 3 = 0$

We subtracted 3 a total of **4 times** $\rightarrow 12 \div 3 = $ **4**

Practice Problems:

1. $12 \div 3 =$

2. $15 \div 5 =$

3. $20 \div 4 =$

4. $18 \div 6 =$

5. $10 \div 2 =$

Reflection:

Take a moment to review the Biblical focus for this section. What does that Bible verse mean to you, and how can you live it or relate to the math concepts learned in this lesson?

_____

_____

_____

_____

_____

Lesson 2: Division Facts and Strategies

Biblical Focus:

"The fear of the Lord is the beginning of wisdom, and knowledge of the Holy One is understanding." – Proverbs 9:10

Learning your division facts is part of gaining wisdom and knowledge. God blesses us when we grow in understanding.

Lesson Objective:

Students will strengthen division fact fluency using multiplication relationships.

Example:

$36 \div 6$

Ask: What number multiplied by 6 equals 36?

Answer: $6 \times 6 = 36 \rightarrow$ So $36 \div 6 = \textbf{6}$

Practice Problems:

1. $36 \div 6 =$

2. $49 \div 7 =$

3. $81 \div 9 =$

4. $64 \div 8 =$

5. $45 \div 5 =$

Reflection:

Take a moment to review the Biblical focus for this section. What does that Bible verse mean to you, and how can you live it or relate to the math concepts learned in this lesson?

_____

_____

_____

_____

_____

Lesson 3: Dividing by 1-Digit Numbers

Biblical Focus:

"Be strong and courageous. Do not be afraid; do not be discouraged, for the Lord your God will be with you wherever you go." – Joshua 1:9

Division can feel intimidating, but we can face challenges with confidence when we trust that God is with us.

Lesson Objective:

Students will divide larger numbers by single-digit divisors using place value and mental math.

Example:

$96 \div 8 =$

Use mental math or long division. Since $8 \times 12 = 96 \rightarrow$ Answer: **12**

Practice Problems:

1. $96 \div 8 =$

2. $72 \div 6 =$

3. $84 \div 7 =$

4. $56 \div 4 =$

5. $36 \div 3 =$

Reflection:

Take a moment to review the Biblical focus for this section. What does that Bible verse mean to you, and how can you live it or relate to the math concepts learned in this lesson?

_____

_____

_____

_____

_____

Lesson 4: Estimating Quotients

Biblical Focus:

"Suppose one of you wants to build a tower. Won't you first sit down and estimate the cost?" – Luke 14:28

God teaches us to plan wisely before taking action. Estimating helps us check our direction before finishing a task.

Lesson Objective:

Students will estimate quotients by rounding dividends and divisors to nearby compatible numbers.

Example:

Estimate: 91 ÷ 9

91 is close to 90, and 90 ÷ 9 = **10** → Estimated answer: **10**

Practice Problems:

1. Estimate: 91 ÷ 9

2. Estimate: 76 ÷ 8

3. Estimate: 43 ÷ 5

4. Estimate: 119 ÷ 6

5. Estimate: $67 \div 4$

Reflection:

Take a moment to review the Biblical focus for this section. What does that Bible verse mean to you, and how can you live it or relate to the math concepts learned in this lesson?

_____

_____

_____

_____

_____

Lesson 5: Division Word Problems

Biblical Focus:

"Each of you should use whatever gift you have received to serve others." – 1 Peter 4:10

Solving division problems in everyday life helps us be good stewards and care for others by thinking clearly and sharing wisely.

Lesson Objective:

Students will apply division to solve real-world word problems involving equal groups and sharing.

Example:

There are 24 pencils divided into 6 boxes.

24 ÷ 6 = **4 pencils per box**

Practice Problems:

1. 24 pencils are packed into 6 boxes. How many per box?

2. 30 cookies are shared among 5 kids. How many of each?

3. 18 apples are placed into 3 baskets. How many apples per basket?

4. 40 chairs are arranged equally at 8 tables. How many chairs per table?

5. 45 books are placed on 9 shelves. How many books are on each shelf?

Reflection:

Take a moment to review the Biblical focus for this section. What does that Bible verse mean to you, and how can you live it or relate to the math concepts learned in this lesson?

_____

_____

_____

_____

_____

Answer Key For Unit 4: Division

Lesson 1: Understanding Division as Repeated Subtraction

1. **12 ÷ 3 = 4**

   Subtract 3 repeatedly from 12: 12 → 9 → 6 → 3 → 0. Four subtractions = 4.

2. **15 ÷ 5 = 3**

   Subtract 5 three times from 15: 15 → 10 → 5 → 0.

3. **20 ÷ 4 = 5**

   Subtract 4 from 20 five times: 20 → 16 → 12 → 8 → 4 → 0.

4. **18 ÷ 6 = 3**

   Subtract 6 from 18: 18 → 12 → 6 → 0. Three steps.

5. **10 ÷ 2 = 5**

   Subtract 2 five times from 10: 10 → 8 → 6 → 4 → 2 → 0.

Lesson 2: Division Facts and Strategies

1. **36 ÷ 6 = 6**

   6 times 6 is 36. Use multiplication facts to solve.

2. **49 ÷ 7 = 7**

   7 times 7 is 49. Recognize the fact family.

3. **81 ÷ 9 = 9**

   9 × 9 = 81. Use known division/multiplication pairs.

Leif The Lion Education

4. **64 ÷ 8 = 8**

   $8 \times 8 = 64$. Solve by fact recall.

5. **45 ÷ 5 = 9**

   $5 \times 9 = 45$. Use multiplication facts to divide.

Lesson 3: Dividing by 1-Digit Numbers

1. **96 ÷ 8 = 12**

   Use long division or recall $8 \times 12 = 96$.

2. **72 ÷ 6 = 12**

   $6 \times 12 = 72$. Divide using known multiplication facts.

3. **84 ÷ 7 = 12**

   $7 \times 12 = 84$. Use multiplication knowledge to divide.

4. **56 ÷ 4 = 14**

   $4 \times 14 = 56$. Divide evenly by grouping.

5. **36 ÷ 3 = 12**

   $3 \times 12 = 36$. Use math facts.

Lesson 4: Estimating Quotients

1. **91 ÷ 9 ≈ 90 ÷ 9 = 10**

   Round 91 to 90 for a quick estimate.

2. **76 ÷ 8 ≈ 80 ÷ 8 = 10**

   Round 76 to 80 and divide.

Leif The Lion Education

3. $43 \div 5 \approx 45 \div 5 = 9$

   45 is close to 43; divide to estimate.

4. $119 \div 6 \approx 120 \div 6 = 20$

   Estimate by rounding 119 to 120.

5. $67 \div 4 \approx 68 \div 4 = 17$

   Estimate with a nearby compatible number.

Lesson 5: Division Word Problems

1. **$24 \div 6 = 4$ pencils per box**

   Equal grouping of pencils into boxes.

2. **$30 \div 5 = 6$ cookies per child**

   Fairly divide cookies among children.

3. **$18 \div 3 = 6$ apples per basket**

   Equal sharing of apples into 3 baskets.

4. **$40 \div 8 = 5$ chairs per table**

   Divide chairs evenly among tables.

5. **$45 \div 9 = 5$ books per shelf**

   Distribute books evenly on shelves.

UNIT 5: FRACTIONS

- Understanding Fractions as Part of a Whole

- Equivalent Fractions

- Comparing and Ordering Fractions

- Adding and Subtracting Like Fractions

- Understanding Mixed Numbers and Improper Fractions

Leif The Lion Education

Lesson 1: Understanding Fractions as Part of a Whole

Biblical Focus:

"We who are many form one body, and each member belongs to all the others." –
Romans 12:5

Fractions show how different parts make up a whole, just like each person plays a part
in God's family.

Lesson Objective:

Students will understand fractions as parts of a whole using visual models and simple
division.

Example:

If a circle is divided into 2 equal parts and 1 part is shaded, then the fraction is **1/2**.

Practice Problems:

1. A shape is divided into 2 parts. One part is shaded. What is the fraction?

2. A square has 4 parts shaded out of 4. What is the fraction?

3. A bar is split into 3 parts, and 2 are shaded. What is the fraction?

4. One piece out of 5 is shaded. Write the fraction.

5. 4 parts are shaded from 6 equal parts. What is the fraction?

Reflection:

Take a moment to review the Biblical focus for this section. What does that Bible verse mean to you, and how can you live it or relate to the math concepts learned in this lesson?

_____

_____

_____

_____

_____

Lesson 2: Equivalent Fractions

Biblical Focus:

"For God shows no partiality." – Romans 2:11

Even when things look different, their value can be the same. Equivalent fractions remind us that what's inside matters most.

Lesson Objective:

Students will identify and create equivalent fractions using models and multiplication/division.

Example:

1/2 = 2/4

Multiply both the numerator and the denominator by 2: $(1×2)/(2×2) = 2/4$

Practice Problems:

1. Is 2/4 equal to 1/2?

2. Is 3/6 equivalent to 1/2?

3. Is 4/8 the same as 1/2?

4. Is 5/10 equal to 1/2?

5. Is 6/12 the same as 1/2?

Reflection:

Take a moment to review the Biblical focus for this section. What does that Bible verse mean to you, and how can you live it or relate to the math concepts learned in this lesson?

_____

_____

_____

_____

_____

Lesson 3: Comparing and Ordering Fractions

Biblical Focus:

"Do not judge by appearances, but judge with right judgment." – John 7:24

Sometimes one fraction looks bigger, but it isn't. God wants us to think carefully before deciding what is greater or smaller.

Lesson Objective:

Students will compare and order fractions with like and unlike denominators.

Example:

Which is bigger: 1/2 or 3/4?

Convert 1/2 to 2/4. Compare: 2/4 < 3/4 → So, **1/2 < 3/4**

Practice Problems:

1. Is 1/2 less than 3/4?

2. Which is greater: 2/3 or 1/3?

3. Compare: 3/8 and 1/2

4. Which is larger: 5/6 or 3/4?

5. Is 1/5 smaller than 1/2?

Leif The Lion Education

Reflection:

Take a moment to review the Biblical focus for this section. What does that Bible verse mean to you, and how can you live it or relate to the math concepts learned in this lesson?

_____

_____

_____

_____

_____

Lesson 4: Adding and Subtracting Like Fractions

Biblical Focus:

"Carry each other's burdens, and in this way you will fulfill the law of Christ." – Galatians 6:2

Adding and subtracting fractions shows how we can share or give. In life and math, this helps us support each other.

Lesson Objective:

Students will add and subtract fractions with like denominators.

Example:

1/4 + 2/4 = 3/4

Add the numerators: 1 + 2 = 3. The denominator stays the same.

Practice Problems:

1. 1/4 + 2/4 =

2. 3/5 – 1/5 =

3. 2/8 + 5/8 =

4. 6/7 – 2/7 =

5. 4/10 + 3/10 =

Reflection:

Take a moment to review the Biblical focus for this section. What does that Bible verse mean to you, and how can you live it or relate to the math concepts learned in this lesson?

_____

_____

_____

_____

_____

Lesson 5: Understanding Mixed Numbers and Improper Fractions

Biblical Focus:

"My grace is sufficient for you, for my power is made perfect in weakness." – 2 Corinthians 12:9

Even when things feel like they're overflowing—like an improper fraction—God brings balance and order.

Lesson Objective:

Students will convert between improper fractions and mixed numbers.

Example:

3/2 → 1 1/2

Two goes into three once with one leftover. Final answer: **1 1/2**

Practice Problems:

1. Convert 3/2 to a mixed number.

2. Change 7/3 to a mixed number.

3. Change 7/4 to a mixed number.

4. Convert 2 1/2 to an improper fraction.

Leif The Lion Education

5. Convert 2 1/4 to an improper fraction.

Reflection:

Take a moment to review the Biblical focus for this section. What does that Bible verse mean to you, and how can you live it or relate to the math concepts learned in this lesson?

_____

_____

_____

_____

_____

Answer Key For Unit 5: Fractions

Lesson 1: Understanding Fractions as Part of a Whole

1. **1/2** – One part is shaded out of two equal parts.

2. **3/4** – Three parts are shaded out of four.

3. **2/3** – Two parts are shaded out of three total parts.

4. **1/5** – One out of five parts is shaded.

5. **4/6** – Four parts are shaded from six equal parts.

Lesson 2: Equivalent Fractions

1. **2/4 = 1/2** – Divide both the numerator and denominator by 2.

2. **3/6 = 1/2** – Divide both by 3.

3. **4/8 = 1/2** – Divide both by 4.

4. **5/10 = 1/2** – Divide both by 5.

5. **6/12 = 1/2** – Divide both by 6.

Leif The Lion Education

Lesson 3: Comparing and Ordering Fractions

1. **1/2 < 3/4** – 2/4 is less than 3/4.

2. **2/3 > 1/3** – Same denominators, compare numerators.

3. **3/8 < 1/2** – 1/2 is 4/8, which is greater than 3/8.

4. **5/6 > 3/4** – Convert to the same denominators or decimals: 0.833 > 0.75.

5. **1/5 < 1/2** – Smaller part of the whole.

Lesson 4: Adding and Subtracting Like Fractions

1. **1/4 + 2/4 = 3/4** – Add numerators; keep denominator.

2. **3/5 − 1/5 = 2/5** – Subtract numerators.

3. **2/8 + 5/8 = 7/8** – Add top numbers.

4. **6/7 − 2/7 = 4/7** – Subtract numerators.

5. **4/10 + 3/10 = 7/10** – Add numerators.

Lesson 5: Understanding Mixed Numbers and Improper Fractions

Leif The Lion Education

1. **3/2 = 1 1/2** – 2 fits in 3 once with 1 leftover.

2. **7/3 = 2 1/3** – 3 goes into 7 twice with 1 leftover.

3. **7/4 = 1 3/4** – 4 goes into 7 once with 3 leftover.

4. **2 1/2 = 5/2** – Multiply 2 × 2 = 4, then add 1 → 5/2.

5. **2 1/4 = 9/4** – Multiply 2 × 4 = 8, then add 1 → 9/4.

UNIT 6: DECIMALS

0.1 **0.87**

- **Understanding Tenths and Hundredths**

- **Reading and Writing Decimals**

- **Comparing and Ordering Decimals**

- **Rounding Decimals**

- **Adding and Subtracting Decimals**

Praise God from whom all blessings flow

Leif The Lion Education

Lesson 1: Understanding Tenths and Hundredths

Biblical Focus:

"Even the very hairs of your head are all numbered." – Matthew 10:30

God cares about the smallest details. Decimals help us see the value in the tiniest parts, just like God values every detail of our lives.

Lesson Objective:

Students will understand decimals as parts of a whole, including tenths and hundredths.

Example:

If a square is divided into 10 equal parts and 1 is shaded, the decimal is **0.1**.

If 25 parts out of 100 are shaded, the decimal is **0.25**.

Practice Problems:

1. What is the decimal for 1 part out of 10?

2. What is the decimal for 5 parts out of 10?

3. What is the decimal for 1 part out of 100?

4. What decimal represents 25 out of 100?

5. What decimal shows 4 parts shaded out of 10?

Reflection:

Take a moment to review the Biblical focus for this section. What does that Bible verse mean to you, and how can you live it or relate to the math concepts learned in this lesson?

_____

_____

_____

_____

_____

Lesson 2: Reading and Writing Decimals

Biblical Focus:

"Let your conversation be always full of grace, seasoned with salt." – Colossians 4:6

Just as we should speak with clarity, we should write numbers with accuracy. Decimals help us communicate value.

Lesson Objective:

Students will learn to read and write decimals in word form and standard form.

Example:

0.3 is read as "three tenths"

0.07 is "seven hundredths"

Practice Problems:

1. Write "three tenths" as a decimal.

2. Write "seven hundredths" as a decimal.

3. What is the word form of 0.48?

4. What is the word form of 0.90?

5. Write "two hundredths" as a decimal.

Reflection:

Take a moment to review the Biblical focus for this section. What does that Bible verse mean to you, and how can you live it or relate to the math concepts learned in this lesson?

_____

_____

_____

_____

_____

Lesson 3: Comparing and Ordering Decimals

Biblical Focus:

"The Lord does not look at the things people look at... the Lord looks at the heart." – 1 Samuel 16:7

Decimals teach us to look carefully. What seems close can be very different. We must learn to compare with wisdom and accuracy.

Lesson Objective:

Students will compare and order decimals to the tenths and hundredths using place value.

Example:

Compare 0.3 and 0.5 → Look at the tenths: 3 < 5, so **0.3 < 0.5**

Practice Problems:

1. Which is greater: 0.3 or 0.5?

2. Which is greater: 0.46 or 0.4?

3. Which is smaller: 0.2 or 0.25?

4. Which is greater: 0.9 or 0.89?

5. Which is smaller: 0.32 or 0.35?

Reflection:

Take a moment to review the Biblical focus for this section. What does that Bible verse mean to you, and how can you live it or relate to the math concepts learned in this lesson?

_____

_____

_____

_____

_____

Lesson 4: Rounding Decimals

Biblical Focus:

"Walk in wisdom toward outsiders, making the best use of the time." – Colossians 4:5

Rounding helps us make quick, wise decisions. It's like focusing on the big picture when small details aren't needed.

Lesson Objective:

Students will round decimals to the nearest tenth using place value understanding.

Example:

0.46 rounds to **0.5** because the hundredths digit (6) is 5 or more.

Practice Problems:

1. Round 0.46 to the nearest tenth.

2. Round 0.33 to the nearest tenth.

3. Round 0.87 to the nearest tenth.

4. Round 0.12 to the nearest tenth.

5. Round 0.28 to the nearest tenth.

Reflection:

Take a moment to review the Biblical focus for this section. What does that Bible verse mean to you, and how can you live it or relate to the math concepts learned in this lesson?

_____

_____

_____

_____

_____

Lesson 5: Adding and Subtracting Decimals

Biblical Focus:

"Two are better than one... If either of them falls down, one can help the other up." –
Ecclesiastes 4:9–10

When decimals are added or subtracted, they work together to show value. Math, like
people, is stronger in unity.

Lesson Objective:

Students will add and subtract decimals to the hundredths place with place value
alignment.

Example:

$0.2 + 0.3 = \mathbf{0.5} \rightarrow$ Line up the decimals before adding.

Practice Problems:

1. $0.2 + 0.3 =$

2. $0.6 - 0.1 =$

3. $0.75 + 0.25 =$

4. $0.9 - 0.4 =$

Leif The Lion Education

5. 0.52 + 0.18 =

Reflection:

Take a moment to review the Biblical focus for this section. What does that Bible verse mean to you, and how can you live it or relate to the math concepts learned in this lesson?

_____

_____

_____

_____

_____

Answer Key for Unit 6: Decimals

Lesson 1: Understanding Tenths and Hundredths

1. **0.1** – One part out of ten is written as 0.1.

2. **0.5** – Five out of ten parts equals 0.5.

3. **0.01** – One part out of one hundred is 0.01.

4. **0.25** – Twenty-five hundredths is written as 0.25.

5. **0.4** – Four tenths is 0.4.

Lesson 2: Reading and Writing Decimals

1. **0.3** – "Three tenths" is written as 0.3.

2. **0.07** – "Seven hundredths" is written as 0.07.

3. **Forty-eight hundredths** – 0.48 is read this way.

4. **Ninety hundredths or nine tenths** – 0.90 can be read either way.

5. **0.02** – "Two hundredths" is written as 0.02.

Leif The Lion Education

Lesson 3: Comparing and Ordering Decimals

1. **0.3 < 0.5** – Tenths place shows 3 is less than 5.

2. **0.46 > 0.4** – Compare hundredths: 46 is greater than 40.

3. **0.2 < 0.25** – 0.20 is less than 0.25.

4. **0.9 > 0.89** – Nine tenths is greater than 89 hundredths.

5. **0.32 < 0.35** – Thirty-two hundredths is less than thirty-five hundredths.

Lesson 4: Rounding Decimals

1. **0.46 → 0.5** – Round up since 6 in hundredths is 5 or more.

2. **0.33 → 0.3** – Round down since 3 in hundredths is less than 5.

3. **0.87 → 0.9** – Round up to 0.9.

4. **0.12 → 0.1** – Round down since hundredths is less than 5.

5. **0.28 → 0.3** – Round up to nearest tenth.

Lesson 5: Adding and Subtracting Decimals

1. **0.2 + 0.3 = 0.5** – Add tenths directly.

2. **0.6 − 0.1 = 0.5** – Subtract tenths.

Leif The Lion Education

3. **0.75 + 0.25 = 1.0** – Add hundredths for one whole.

4. **0.9 − 0.4 = 0.5** – Subtract tenths.

5. **0.52 + 0.18 = 0.70** – Add hundredths, carry if needed.

UNIT 7: MEASUREMENT

Measuring Length (U.S. Customary and Metric)

- Measuring Weight and Mass
- Measuring Capacity
- Solving Measurement Word Problems
- Converting Units of Measurement
- Checking for Reasonableness

Leif The Lion Education

Lesson 1: Measuring Length (U.S. Customary and Metric)

Biblical Focus:

"You have set a boundary that they may not pass over, that they may not return to cover the earth." – Psalm 104:9

God sets boundaries in nature, just as we measure and define lengths with tools He's given us.

Lesson Objective:

Students will understand and convert between common units of length in both customary and metric systems.

Example:

12 inches = 1 foot

1 meter = 100 centimeters

Practice Problems:

1. How many inches are in a foot?

2. How many feet are in a yard?

3. How many centimeters are in a meter?

4. Convert 5 kilometers to meters.

Leif The Lion Education

5. How many inches are in 3 feet?

Reflection:

Take a moment to review the Biblical focus for this section. What does that Bible verse mean to you, and how can you live it or relate to the math concepts learned in this lesson?

_____

_____

_____

_____

_____

Lesson 2: Measuring Weight and Mass

Biblical Focus:

"A false balance is an abomination to the Lord, but a just weight is His delight." – Proverbs 11:1

God values fairness. Accurate weights help us stay honest and reflect His truth in our daily lives.

Lesson Objective:

Students will learn to identify and convert between customary and metric units of weight and mass.

Example:

16 ounces = 1 pound

1 kilogram = 1,000 grams

Practice Problems:

1. How many ounces are in a pound?

2. How many ounces are in 2 pounds?

3. How many grams are in a kilogram?

4. Convert 4 pounds to ounces.

5. Convert 3 kilograms to grams.

Leif The Lion Education

Reflection:

Take a moment to review the Biblical focus for this section. What does that Bible verse mean to you, and how can you live it or relate to the math concepts learned in this lesson?

_____

_____

_____

_____

_____

Lesson 3: Measuring Capacity

Biblical Focus:

"My cup overflows with blessings." – Psalm 23:5

Understanding capacity reminds us of God's abundant blessings. We measure what overflows so we can share wisely.

Lesson Objective:

Students will measure and convert units of capacity in the U.S. customary and metric systems.

Example:

8 fluid ounces = 1 cup

1 liter = 1,000 milliliters

Practice Problems:

1. How many fluid ounces are in a cup?

2. How many cups are in a pint?

3. How many quarts are in a gallon?

4. How many milliliters are in a liter?

5. How many quarts are in 2 gallons?

Reflection:

Take a moment to review the Biblical focus for this section. What does that Bible verse mean to you, and how can you live it or relate to the math concepts learned in this lesson?

_____

_____

_____

_____

_____

Lesson 4: Solving Measurement Word Problems

Biblical Focus:

"Let all things be done decently and in order." – 1 Corinthians 14:40

Solving problems with units helps us keep life organized and useful. God loves order in all things.

Lesson Objective:

Students will apply unit conversions to real-world problems involving length, weight, and capacity.

Example:

How many inches are in 5 feet?

Answer: 5 × 12 = **60 inches**

Practice Problems:

1. A rope is 5 feet long. How many inches is that?

2. You pour 4 cups of juice. How many pints is that?

3. A table is 2 yards long. How many feet?

4. How many quarts are in 3 gallons of water?

5. Convert 1.5 liters to milliliters.

Reflection:

Take a moment to review the Biblical focus for this section. What does that Bible verse mean to you, and how can you live it or relate to the math concepts learned in this lesson?

_____

_____

_____

_____

_____

Lesson 5: Converting Units of Measurement

Biblical Focus:

"Teach us to number our days, that we may gain a heart of wisdom." – Psalm 90:12

Measuring helps us manage our time, energy, and resources wisely. Learning conversions is part of good stewardship.

Lesson Objective:

Students will convert between larger and smaller units using multiplication and division.

Example:

36 inches = 3 feet (divide by 12)

4 feet = 48 inches (multiply by 12)

Practice Problems:

1. Convert 36 inches to feet.

2. Convert 2,000 milliliters to liters.

3. Convert 4 feet to inches.

4. Convert 1.2 kilograms to grams.

5. Convert 8 cups to fluid ounces.

Reflection:

Take a moment to review the Biblical focus for this section. What does that Bible verse mean to you, and how can you live it or relate to the math concepts learned in this lesson?

_____

_____

_____

_____

_____

Answer Key for Unit 7: Measurement

Lesson 1: Measuring Length (U.S. Customary and Metric)

1. **12 inches = 1 foot** – This is a standard U.S. customary conversion.

2. **3 feet = 1 yard** – One yard equals three feet.

3. **1 meter ≈ 100 centimeters** – Metric system rule.

4. **5 kilometers = 5,000 meters** – Multiply kilometers by 1,000.

5. **36 inches = 3 feet** – Divide 36 by 12 to convert to feet.

Lesson 2: Measuring Weight and Mass

1. **16 ounces = 1 pound** – U.S. customary units of weight.

2. **2 pounds = 32 ounces** – Multiply 2 × 16.

3. **1 kilogram = 1,000 grams** – Metric unit conversion.

4. **4 pounds = 64 ounces** – 4 × 16 = 64.

5. **3 kilograms = 3,000 grams** – Multiply by 1,000.

Leif The Lion Education

Lesson 3: Measuring Capacity

1. **8 fluid ounces = 1 cup** – Common U.S. measurement.

2. **2 cups = 1 pint** – There are 2 cups in 1 pint.

3. **4 quarts = 1 gallon** – Four quarts make up a gallon.

4. **1 liter = 1,000 milliliters** – Standard metric conversion.

5. **2 gallons = 8 quarts** – Multiply 2×4.

Lesson 4: Solving Measurement Word Problems

1. **5 feet = 60 inches** – Multiply 5×12 inches per foot.

2. **4 cups = 2 pints** – Two cups in a pint, so divide 4 by 2.

3. **2 yards = 6 feet** – Each yard equals 3 feet.

4. **3 gallons = 12 quarts** – Multiply 3×4.

5. **1.5 liters = 1,500 milliliters** – Multiply $1.5 \times 1,000$.

Lesson 5: Converting Units of Measurement

1. **36 inches = 3 feet** – Divide by 12.

Leif The Lion Education

2. **2,000 milliliters = 2 liters** – Divide by 1,000.

3. **4 feet = 48 inches** – Multiply 4 × 12.

4. **1.2 kilograms = 1,200 grams** – Multiply by 1,000.

5. **8 cups = 64 fluid ounces** – Multiply 8 × 8.

Unit 8: Geometry

- Identifying Points, Lines, and Angles
- Classifying Triangles and Quadrilaterals
- Lines of Symmetry
- Measuring Angles with a Protractor
- Perimeter and Area

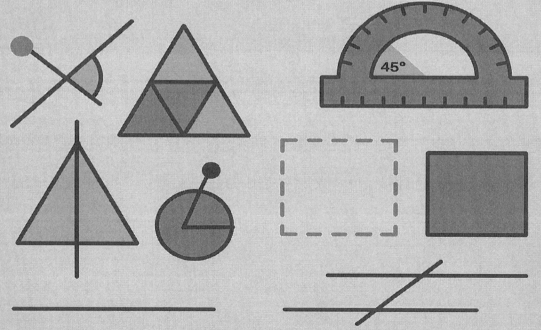

Leif The Lion Education

Lesson 1: Identifying Points, Lines, and Angles

Biblical Focus:

"He marks out the horizon on the face of the waters for a boundary between light and darkness." – Job 26:10

God created the world with shape, direction, and beauty. Geometry reminds us of the precision of His design.

Lesson Objective:

Students will identify points, lines, line segments, and types of angles.

Example:

- A **point** is a location (like a dot).

- A **line** continues in both directions with no end.

- A **line segment** has two endpoints.

- A **right angle** forms a square corner (90°).

Practice Problems:

1. What is a point in geometry?

2. What is a line?

3. What is a line segment?

4. What angle measures exactly 90 degrees?

5. What is an acute angle?

Reflection:

Take a moment to review the Biblical focus for this section. What does that Bible verse mean to you, and how can you live it or relate to the math concepts learned in this lesson?

_____

_____

_____

_____

_____

Lesson 2: Classifying Triangles and Quadrilaterals

Biblical Focus:

"By wisdom the Lord laid the earth's foundations, by understanding he set the heavens in place." – Proverbs 3:19

Shapes help us understand the structure of God's creation. Everything has order, purpose, and design.

Lesson Objective:

Students will identify and classify triangles and quadrilaterals by their sides and angles.

Example:

- A triangle with all equal sides is **equilateral**.

- A **right triangle** has one 90° angle.

- A **square** has four equal sides and right angles.

- A **rectangle** has opposite sides equal and four right angles.

Practice Problems:

1. What is an equilateral triangle?

2. What type of triangle has one right angle?

3. Name a quadrilateral with 4 equal sides and 4 right angles.

4. What shape has opposite sides equal and 4 right angles?

5. What shape has all equal sides but may not have right angles?

Reflection:

Take a moment to review the Biblical focus for this section. What does that Bible verse mean to you, and how can you live it or relate to the math concepts learned in this lesson?

_____

_____

_____

_____

_____

Lesson 3: Lines of Symmetry

Biblical Focus:

"For God is not a God of disorder but of peace." – 1 Corinthians 14:33

Symmetry reminds us that God brings balance and beauty into all things, including us.

Lesson Objective:

Students will identify lines of symmetry in two-dimensional shapes.

Example:

- A square has **4** lines of symmetry.

- A circle has **infinite** lines of symmetry.

- A heart has **1** line of symmetry.

Practice Problems:

1. How many lines of symmetry does a square have?

2. How many lines of symmetry does a rectangle have?

3. How many lines of symmetry does a circle have?

4. How many lines of symmetry does an equilateral triangle have?

5. How many lines of symmetry does a heart have?

Reflection:

Take a moment to review the Biblical focus for this section. What does that Bible verse mean to you, and how can you live it or relate to the math concepts learned in this lesson?

_____

_____

_____

_____

_____

Lesson 4: Measuring Angles with a Protractor

Biblical Focus:

"Make level paths for your feet and take only ways that are firm." – Proverbs 4:26

Angles guide direction and choices, just like God's Word gives direction for our lives.

Lesson Objective:

Students will measure angles using a protractor and identify them as acute, right, or obtuse.

Example:

- **Right angle** = 90°

- **Acute angle** = less than 90°

- **Obtuse angle** = more than 90° but less than 180°

Practice Problems:

1. What type of angle measures 90 degrees?

2. What is an angle that measures 45 degrees?

3. What is an angle that measures 135 degrees?

Leif The Lion Education   117

4. What is the name of a 180-degree angle?

5. What kind of angle is 60 degrees?

Reflection:

Take a moment to review the Biblical focus for this section. What does that Bible verse mean to you, and how can you live it or relate to the math concepts learned in this lesson?

_____

_____

_____

_____

_____

Lesson 5: Perimeter and Area

Biblical Focus:

"Lengthen your cords, strengthen your stakes." – Isaiah 54:2

God teaches us to stretch and build with purpose. Understanding area and perimeter helps us prepare wisely.

Lesson Objective:

Students will calculate the perimeter and area of squares and rectangles using formulas.

Example:

- **Perimeter of square** = 4 + 4 + 4 + 4 = 16 units

- **Area of a rectangle** = length × width

- **Area of a square** = side × side

Practice Problems:

1. Find the perimeter of a square with sides of 4 units.

2. What is the area of a rectangle that is 5 units long and 3 units wide?

3. What is the perimeter of a rectangle that is 6 units long and 2 units wide?

4. Find the area of a square with a side length of 6.

5. Find the area of a rectangle that is 7 units by 4 units.

Reflection:

Take a moment to review the Biblical focus for this section. What does that Bible verse mean to you, and how can you live it or relate to the math concepts learned in this lesson?

_____

_____

_____

_____

_____

Answer Key for Unit 8: Geometry

Lesson 1: Identifying Points, Lines, and Angles

1. A point shows a location, usually marked with a dot.

2. A line extends forever in both directions.

3. A line segment has two endpoints and does not continue.

4. A right angle measures 90 degrees.

5. An acute angle is less than 90 degrees.

Lesson 2: Classifying Triangles and Quadrilaterals

1. An equilateral triangle has all sides of the same length.

2. A right triangle has one angle that measures 90 degrees.

3. A square has four equal sides and four right angles.

4. A rectangle has opposite sides equal and four right angles.

5. A rhombus has four equal sides but doesn't need right angles.

Leif The Lion Education

Lesson 3: Lines of Symmetry

1. A square has 4 lines of symmetry.

2. A rectangle has 2 lines of symmetry.

3. A circle has infinite lines of symmetry.

4. An equilateral triangle has 3 lines of symmetry.

5. A heart has 1 line of symmetry (vertical).

Lesson 4: Measuring Angles with a Protractor

1. A right angle measures 90 degrees.

2. A 45-degree angle is acute.

3. A 135-degree angle is obtuse.

4. A straight angle measures 180 degrees.

5. A 60-degree angle is acute.

Lesson 5: Perimeter and Area

1. Perimeter = 4 + 4 + 4 + 4 = 16 units.

Leif The Lion Education

2. Area = 5 × 3 = 15 square units.

3. Perimeter = 2 × (6 + 2) = 16 units.

4. Area = 6 × 6 = 36 square units.

5. Area = 7 × 4 = 28 square units.

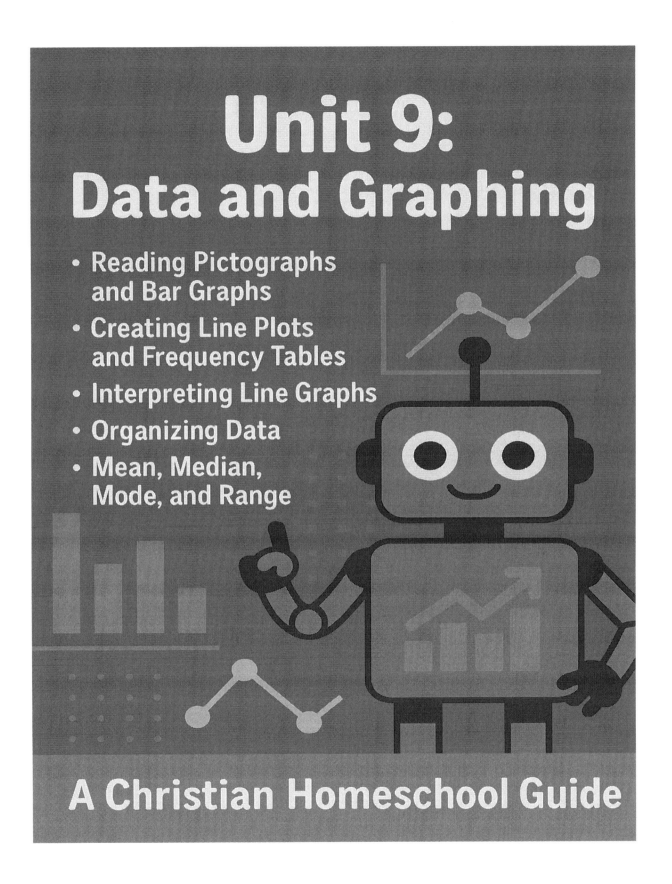

Unit 9:
Data and Graphing

- Reading Pictographs and Bar Graphs
- Creating Line Plots and Frequency Tables
- Interpreting Line Graphs
- Organizing Data
- Mean, Median, Mode, and Range

A Christian Homeschool Guide

Leif The Lion Education

Lesson 1: Reading Pictographs and Bar Graphs

Biblical Focus:

"The Lord sees not as man sees: man looks on the outward appearance, but the Lord looks on the heart." – 1 Samuel 16:7

Graphs show us a picture of information, but we must also look deeper to understand the meaning, just like God looks beyond appearances.

Lesson Objective:

Students will read and interpret data using pictographs and bar graphs.

Example:

If a pictograph shows 4 stars and each star represents 5 votes, the total is 4 × 5 = **20 votes**.

Practice Problems:

1. What does each picture or bar show in a graph?

2. A pictograph has 4 pictures. Each represents 5. What's the total?

3. Which item was chosen most if its bar is the tallest?

4. If each symbol equals 10 and there are 3 symbols, what is the total?

5. How do you find the number of books read using the bar labeled "Books"?

Reflection:

Take a moment to review the Biblical focus for this section. What does that Bible verse mean to you, and how can you live it or relate to the math concepts learned in this lesson?

_____

_____

_____

_____

_____

Lesson 2: Creating Line Plots and Frequency Tables

Biblical Focus:

"Let all things be done decently and in order." – 1 Corinthians 14:40

When we organize data, we bring clarity and peace to information, just as God brings order to the world.

Lesson Objective:

Students will create line plots and frequency tables to represent data sets.

Example:

Scores: 90, 90, 90, 90 → Line plot has four Xs above 90.

Frequency table for 1, 2, 2, 3 →

1 = 1 time, 2 = 2 times, 3 = 1 time.

Practice Problems:

1. Create a line plot using tally data.

2. How do you count values in a frequency table?

3. If 4 students scored 90, how many Xs are above 90?

4. Data set: 1, 2, 2, 3 – What's the frequency of each number?

5. On a line plot, what number has the most Xs?

Reflection:

Take a moment to review the Biblical focus for this section. What does that Bible verse mean to you, and how can you live it or relate to the math concepts learned in this lesson?

_____

_____

_____

_____

_____

Lesson 3: Interpreting Line Graphs

Biblical Focus:

"In all your ways acknowledge Him, and He will make your paths straight." – Proverbs 3:6

Line graphs show direction and change over time, like God's guidance helping us stay on the right path.

Lesson Objective:

Students will interpret trends, highs, lows, and patterns in line graphs.

Example:

A steep line means a quick increase or decrease.

The highest point on the graph shows the maximum value.

Practice Problems:

1. What does a rising line mean?

2. What does the highest point on the graph show?

3. What does the steepest part of the graph mean?

4. What does a flat line on a graph represent?

5. What does the lowest point show?

Reflection:

Take a moment to review the Biblical focus for this section. What does that Bible verse mean to you, and how can you live it or relate to the math concepts learned in this lesson?

_____

_____

_____

_____

_____

Lesson 4: Organizing Data

Biblical Focus:

"But everything should be done in a fitting and orderly way." – 1 Corinthians 14:40

Organizing data teaches discipline and thoughtfulness—values that help us live with purpose.

Lesson Objective:

Students will sort, label, and present data using tallies, tables, and charts.

Example:

To organize the set: 3, 1, 2, 2

Order it: 1, 2, 2, 3

Tally:

1 – |

2 – ||

3 – |

Practice Problems:

1. How do you group data to make a chart?

2. Why should you sort numbers before organizing?

3. How can tally marks help?

4. What makes a data table clear and easy to read?

5. How do you summarize data into groups?

Reflection:

Take a moment to review the Biblical focus for this section. What does that Bible verse mean to you, and how can you live it or relate to the math concepts learned in this lesson?

_____

_____

_____

_____

_____

Lesson 5: Mean, Median, Mode, and Range

Biblical Focus:

"Let us examine our ways and test them, and let us return to the Lord." – Lamentations 3:40

Math asks us to examine data closely, just like Scripture invites us to examine our lives with honesty.

Lesson Objective:

Students will calculate and interpret the mean, median, mode, and range of a data set.

Example:

Set: 2, 4, 6

- **Mean** = (2+4+6)/3 = 12/3 = **4**

- **Median** = Middle number = 4

- **Mode** = None (all different)

- **Range** = 6 − 2 = 4

Practice Problems:

1. Find the mean of 2, 4, and 6.

2. What is the median of 3, 5, 7?

3. What is the mode of 1, 2, 2, 3?

4. What is the range of 5, 8, 12?

5. Set: 1, 2, 2, 3 – Find mean, median, mode, and range.

Reflection:

Take a moment to review the Biblical focus for this section. What does that Bible verse mean to you, and how can you live it or relate to the math concepts learned in this lesson?

_____

_____

_____

_____

_____

Answer Key for Unit 9: Data and Graphing

Lesson 1: Reading Pictographs and Bar Graphs

1. Read the key and bar height, or number of pictures.

2. $4 \times 5 = 20$

3. The tallest bar shows the most popular item.

4. 3 symbols $\times$ 10 = 30

5. Look at the height of the bar labeled "Books."

Lesson 2: Creating Line Plots and Frequency Tables

1. Use an X above each number to show how often it appears.

2. Count how many times each value appears.

3. Four students = 4 Xs above 90.

4. Frequencies: 1 = 1, 2 = 2, 3 = 1

5. The number with the most Xs is the most frequent.

Leif The Lion Education

Lesson 3: Interpreting Line Graphs

1. A rising line means an increase.

2. The highest point shows the largest value.

3. The steepest line shows the fastest change.

4. Flat line = no change.

5. The lowest point shows the minimum value.

Lesson 4: Organizing Data

1. Group similar items in rows/columns.

2. Sorting helps see patterns and avoid confusion.

3. Tally marks count items clearly.

4. Label each column; keep spacing even.

5. Divide into categories for better understanding.

Lesson 5: Mean, Median, Mode, and Range

1. $(2+4+6)/3 = 12/3 = 4$

2. The middle of 3, 5, 7 is 5

3. Mode is 2 (appears twice)

4. Range = 12 − 5 = 7

5. Mean = 2, Median = 2, Mode = 2, Range = 2

UNIT 10
PATTERNS AND ALGEBRAIC THINKING

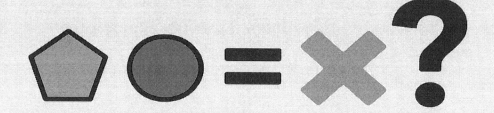

- Identifying Patterns and Sequences
- Solving for Unknowns in Equations
- Writing and Evaluating Expressions
- Using Input-Output Tables
- Problem Solving with Patterns

Leif The Lion Education

Lesson 1: Recognizing and Extending Patterns

Biblical Focus:

"To everything there is a season, and a time for every purpose under heaven." –
Ecclesiastes 3:1

Just like God created seasons with patterns, numbers also follow predictable paths we
can discover and understand.

Lesson Objective:

Students will identify, describe, and extend numeric and visual patterns.

Example:

Pattern: 2, 4, 6, 8. The rule is +2. The next number is **10**.

Practice Problems:

1. What comes next: 2, 4, 6, 8, ___?

2. 1, 2, 4, 8, ___ – What is the rule and next term?

3. Circle, square, circle, square, ___

4. 3, 6, 9, 12, ___ – What is the rule?

5. 30, 25, 20, ____ – What is happening in the pattern?

Reflection:

Take a moment to review the Biblical focus for this section. What does that Bible verse mean to you, and how can you live it or relate to the math concepts learned in this lesson?

_____

_____

_____

_____

_____

Lesson 2: Using Symbols to Represent Unknowns

Biblical Focus:

"The secret things belong to the Lord our God, but the things revealed belong to us and our children forever." – Deuteronomy 29:29

God reveals truth in His time. In math, unknown values are waiting to be discovered by us, too.

Lesson Objective:

Students will use letters or symbols to represent unknown numbers in expressions.

Example:

$x + 5 = 10$

Subtract 5 from both sides → **$x = 5$**

Practice Problems:

1. $x + 5 = 10$ – Find x

2. $7 = y - 3$ – Find y

3. $a - 2 = 8$ – Find a

4. $x \times 4 = 20$ – Find x

5. $36 \div x = 6$ – Find x

Reflection:

Take a moment to review the Biblical focus for this section. What does that Bible verse mean to you, and how can you live it or relate to the math concepts learned in this lesson?

_____

_____

_____

_____

_____

Lesson 3: Solving Simple Equations

Biblical Focus:

"If any of you lacks wisdom, let him ask of God, who gives generously to all without reproach, and it will be given him." – James 1:5

Solving equations is like asking the right question—God provides the answer in His wisdom.

Lesson Objective:

Students will solve one-step equations using addition, subtraction, multiplication, or division.

Example:

$x - 2 = 4 \rightarrow$ Add 2 to both sides $\rightarrow$ **x = 6**

Practice Problems:

1. $x + 3 = 9$

2. $x - 2 = 4$

3. $3x = 12$

4. $x \div 2 = 5$

5. $x - 7 = 0$

Reflection:

Take a moment to review the Biblical focus for this section. What does that Bible verse mean to you, and how can you live it or relate to the math concepts learned in this lesson?

_____

_____

_____

_____

_____

Lesson 4: Number Patterns and Relationships

Biblical Focus:

"For His invisible attributes, His eternal power and divine nature, have been clearly seen, being understood from what has been made." – Romans 1:20

Patterns in creation reveal God's beauty and order. Number patterns reflect the same truths.

Lesson Objective:

Students will identify and analyze patterns in number sequences.

Example:

Squares: 1, 4, 9, 16 → Next is **25**

Practice Problems:

1. 1, 3, 5, 7, ____ – What type of numbers?

2. 2, 4, 6, 8, ____ – What is the pattern?

3. 2, 4, 8, ____ – What is happening here?

4. 3, 6, 9, ____ – What's the rule?

5. 1, 4, 9, 16, ____ – What type of pattern?

Reflection:

Take a moment to review the Biblical focus for this section. What does that Bible verse mean to you, and how can you live it or relate to the math concepts learned in this lesson?

_____

_____

_____

_____

_____

Lesson 5: Real-World Algebra Problems

Biblical Focus:

"Commit to the Lord whatever you do, and your plans will succeed." – Proverbs 16:3

Even when solving everyday problems, trust in God helps us stay clear-minded and focused.

Lesson Objective:

Students will apply algebraic thinking to real-world word problems.

Example:

If you have 5 apples and buy 3 more, the total apples = 5 + 3 = **8**

Practice Problems:

1. You have 5 apples and buy 3 more. How many now?

2. You had $10 and spent $7. How much is left?

3. You have 3 packs of pencils. Each pack has 4 pencils. Total?

4. You share 12 cookies among 4 kids. Each gets how many?

5. You had 9 balloons and gave away 5. How many now?

Reflection:

Take a moment to review the Biblical focus for this section. What does that Bible verse mean to you, and how can you live it or relate to the math concepts learned in this lesson?

_____

_____

_____

_____

_____

Answer Key for Unit 10: Patterns and Algebraic Thinking

Lesson 1: Recognizing and Extending Patterns

1. Add 2 → Next is 10

2. Multiply by 2 → Next is 16

3. Pattern: Circle, square → Next is circle

4. Add 3 → 3, 6, 9, 12 → Next is 15

5. Subtract 5 → 30, 25, 20 → Next is 15

Lesson 2: Using Symbols to Represent Unknowns

1. $x = 5$

2. $y = 10$

3. $a = 10$

4. $x = 5$

5. $x = 6$

Leif The Lion Education

Lesson 3: Solving Simple Equations

1. $x = 6$

2. $x = 6$

3. $x = 4$

4. $x = 10$

5. $x = 7$

Lesson 4: Number Patterns and Relationships

1. Odd numbers → Next is 9

2. Even numbers → Next is 10

3. Doubling → Next is 16

4. Multiply by 3 → Next is 12

5. Square numbers → Next is 25

Lesson 5: Real-World Algebra Problems

1. $5 + 3 = 8$

Leif The Lion Education

2. $10 - 7 = 3$

3. $3 \times 4 =$

4. $12 \div 4 = 3$

5. $9 - 5 = 4$

Made in the USA
Columbia, SC
07 June 2025

59057622R10085